The Night Post

MATTHEW SWEENEY was born in Donegal, Ireland in 1952. He moved to London in 1973 and studied at the Polytechnic of North London and the University of Freiburg. He won a Cholmondeley Award in 1987 and an Arts Council Writer's Award in 1999.

Also by Matthew Sweeney

POETRY

Black Moon
Sanctuary
Selected Poems
A Smell of Fish
The Bridal Suite
Cacti
Blue Shoes
The Lame Waltzer
A Round House
A Dream of Maps

POETRY FOR CHILDREN

Up on the Roof: New and Selected Poems
Fatso in the Red Suit
The Flying Spring Onion

FICTION FOR CHILDREN

Fox
The Snow Vulture

The Night Post

A New Selection

by

MATTHEW SWEENEY

SALT
LONDON

PUBLISHED BY SALT PUBLISHING
Dutch House, 307–308 High Holborn, London WC1V 7LL United Kingdom

Salt Publishing 2010

Printed in Great Britain by the MPG Books Group, Bodmin and King's Lynn

Typeset in Swift 9.5 / 13

ISBN 978 1 907773 01 3 hardback

1 3 5 7 9 8 6 4 2

i.m. my sister Bláithín

Contents

Acknowledgements xiii

THE MOONPOEMS
Fog 1
Winter 2
Nightlights 3
Nightshow 5
Nightfall 7
Shadows 8
Siege 9
Visit 10
Freedom 11
Drought 12
Nightlong 13
Holland Park Walk 14
Deluge 16
'I'm Dreaming of a White Xmas' 18
'Was Hast Du Mit Mond Getan?' 20
ZZZZ 22
Ball 24
Garden 26
Dreams 28
No Welcome 29
Astronomy 30
The Statue 31
Dracula's Cathedral 32
The Birds 33
The Dentist 35
A Round House 37
Holiday 38
Blondbeard 39

The Monks 40
Home 41
The Return 42
A Goodbye to Germany, August 1978 43
Neighbourly Sounds 44
Rain 45
Bad Blood 46
The Window 47
New Town 48
Lili Marlene 50
A Fable 51
The Lake 52
Gifts 54
New Year Party 55
The Servant 57
Electric Nights 59
The Dancehall 60
The Ideal Home 62
The Hole 63
A Crow's Cremation 64
Mr Lu, the Guitarist 65
The Obituarist 66
The Infirmary 67
Variation on a Dream 68
Wild Garlic 69
The Lame Waltzer 70
The Aerial 71
Heirs 73
Split-Level 74
Sarsaparilla 75
The Night Post 76

The Shark	77
Geometry	78
The Mugging	79
The Pitch	80
A Holborn Lamppost	81
In the White City	82
Divers At The Laurentic	83
The Cold	84
The Sea At Pollan	85
Dog On A Chain	88
The Border	89
Digesting Crab Claws	90
The Crab Rock	91
The Lighthouse Keeper's Son	92
Calais	93
Boy With A Rod	95
Hitchhiking	96
Leaving The Surface	98
Dredging The Lake	99
The Statues	100
The Haunt Of The Night-Owl	102
Omelettes	104
No Answer	105
How Witches Went Invisible	106
The Queue	107
Her Song	109
The Coffin Shop	110
A Diary Of Symptoms	111
The Stone Ship	112
Torchlight	114
Singing	115

The Hill 116
The Knowing Birds 117
Whatever 118
Breaches 119
Blue Eggs 120
Bears 121
The Dark 122
Banknotes 123
The Flying Spring Onion 124
Fishbones Dreaming 125
Johnjoe's Snowman 127
Night Boy 128
All the Dogs 130
Me and Benjy 131
Mule 133
While I Practise My Piano 135
Smile 136
The Unlit Suburbs 137
The Long-Legged Chair 140
Sleep With A Suitcase 141
Riding Into Town 142
Grandpa's Bed 143
Writing To A Dead Man 144
Meat 146
Chinese Opera 147
Our Ikky 148
The Mules 150
Donkey Hoof 151
Dancer 152
The Dog 153
Postcards 154

Skylight	155
Keep Him In	156
The Attic	157
The Houseboat	159
Weddings And Funerals	160
A Day In Calcutta	161
The Horses	163
My Daughter And Ray Davies	165
Five Fighters	166
Hooves	167
The Sleeping Sailor	169
Magott Song	170
Permissions	173

Acknowledgements

Acknowledgements are due to editors of the following (many now defunct), where some of the previously uncollected work has appeared:

Aquarius, Clunch, Cracked Lookingglass, Graphein, Green Lines, Green River Review, Icarus, Krino, North Magazine, Pacific Quarterly Moana, Pebble Broadsheet, Poetry Ireland Review, Poetry Review, Profiles, Something Beginning with P, Ulster Tatler.

Otherwise, the poems have previously been included in the following books:

A Dream of Maps (Raven Arts Press), *A Round House* (Allison & Busby/Raven Arts Press), *The Lame Waltzer* (Allison & Busby/Raven Arts Press), *Blue Shoes* (Secker & Warburg), Cacti (Secker & Warburg), *The Flying Spring Onion* (Faber & Faber), *Fatso in the Red Suit* (Faber & Faber), *The Bridal Suite* (Cape Poetry), *A Smell of Fish* (Cape Poetry).

A fuller version of the opening sequence of moonpoems was to have been published by Ian Robinson in his *Oasis Books* series in 1978 till I pulled it. The sequence is dedicated to his memory.

The three little songs that comprise 'The Unlit Suburbs' have been set to music by John Woolrich and appear by permission of Faber Music.

'Maggot Song' was comissioned by Barbican Education, as part of one of their projects.

The Night Post

Fog

Stunned, I emerge to a night
where darkness has a strange sidekick.
Clouds lie fallen on the city.
Armies of giant ghosts
swarm down streets, clap
rows of houses in invisible hoods,
roll in great waves
                    down subterranean railway platforms.

Dim shapes of cars crawl by,
awkward as prototype tanks, freed from museums,
gummy without their guns.

                              My eyes
are almost useless cannibal delicacies.
Lungs ache their disapproval.

Masked like a murderer, I
miraculously find a busstop, peer
lest a 2decked monster rumble by.

And the fogsoldiers close in around me,
hound me with their ghostly fingers.

Their muffled murmurings
                              echo.

Winter

Wind
        has ice on his teeth today.

I hurry through slow streets,
tighten my woollen noose.
                                    Wind hounds me
all the way, finding my fingers, toes
the easiest torment. Often
he snarls behind me.

I am no polarbear, disguised as snow.
I am not even tough. Coat a useless bodyguard,
my very bones are bitten. Hunched together
I bear his bullying in silence.

As I hurry past, houses
leak their warmth through ½ open doors.
My footsteps ring mockingly.
Ghosts of my breath hang mouthhigh,
point treacherously to where I am
lest wind forget.

                        I mount the steps,   but
is that
         moon
                  I see,
frostwhite, clinging to morning,
her final glare
                    faint
through the frozen wastes of space
                                              between us?

Nightlights

No cloud in sight. Wind
pants the wintry arms of trees aside,
lets moon be seen.
She is fat tonight,
an X-ray of a bloated skull
pinned on the huge breast of night.
A ghostly glow escapes her,
stretching.

I feel I'm being watched. Houses
offer temporary cover, then betray me again
to her cold deathglare.
Her sodium sentries line the street,
give their glow as reinforcement. That
is about as bright, as horrible
as a sick sun.

I get a strong stench
of being stared at.
I hurry.

Muffled lights of passing houses
encourage me by their indifference. They
will not be bullied into unsought alliance.

I turn the corner home.
The shopwindow holds moon's reflection,
shocks me with dirty tactics.
Then as my roomlight

beacons across the street, a car
swings round the bend. Its headlights
transfix.

Nightshow

Drunk, my feet play tricks on me,
mutiny & will not walk.
                                        My face
lies from the toilet mirror,
a grinning imposter, & the pissstream
will not stop.
                        Body is playing up again.
Later I must punish it.

                                        I stagger back
through herds at the crowded beerpool.
The closing knell ricochets from walls
with an awful sound.
                                        Too torturous
trying to reach the pool. In my present state
& with such a greedy pressing crowd
I would be trampled underfoot.
                                                    Instead I
grasp my ½ full glass tenderly,
savour each precious drop as if
we'd never meet again,
                                        & lights out
I will not stay to be bawled at.

                                                    Outside
I gulp in great lumps of night.
2 moons play tag across the sky.
                                                    The road
snakes its way between cars, maliciously

humps its serpent back beneath me.

Somehow

I reach home, coax the huge key
into the tiny lock,
flop motionless on the bed.
As I slide away, the growls of a
straining pack of nightmares
meet me at the doors of sleep.
Tomorrow
I will wake, a head chewed to shreds
the only memory.

Nightfall

Fatfaced sun slides red behind the city,
hauls his lightrays behind him. A few
shadows scout about,
then night invades.
The reign of darkness is back.

Moon already haloes freely,
a sick grin carved on her pimpled face.
Greedy for control, she urges the newnight
to my window, demands he enter.

I see him press against the glass.
Only my 2 watchdog lights,
whipped alive by tame lightning,
keep me safe. He will not leave.
Waits outside, the most horrifying of ghosts
peering over his shoulder.

My safety is sabotaged.
Should the electricity fail, I would be finished.
I pull the curtains,
dive trembling
beneath the blankets, begging sleep to save me.

Shadows

Marching grimly, they stay
close as guidedogs,
                                        or executioners.
I cannot lose them. Every
twist brings them too, my
dogged men in black. Sometimes there's 1
—dragging me after him
at a ridiculous pace—but more often
2, 3,
    before, behind. I am trapped
& they will not show their faces.
Profiles show a similarity, & are all
strangely familiar.

                                        I smell treachery.

Moon, I notice, is their dynamo.
That innocent holycommunion
seeps her lifegiving glow
through their black pores.
& her sodium street-thugs
                                                kick strength
into their frail bodies.

                                            They have me now.
Down the footpath they accompany me,
& with every step
                                    my headache howls
louder in anticipation.

Siege

Crouched in a shady corner, I
beat back (not without sweat)
                    the reflection of sunlight.
Sun himself is unthinkable. Oh
for a sneeze from winterwind,
                                        to freeze
in midair those bullying sunarrows,
leaving them brittle.

These saline drops tickling my forehead
tell me
          I have no need to piss
now. I am grateful.

                              I must escape.

Night's secretpassage,
                                moonwatched,
is my best bet. I
will stowaway in an iceberg,
sail, starpropelled, to a southern sea.

Oh, how those cold waves will
                                slurp up sunbeams . . .

Visit

Last outpost of the underground.

I fight my way upsteps,
find wind in angry mood.
                                        Tonight
he does not want me aboveground.
NOONE
            may stroll the streets. Even
the streetlights
                        are cowed,
hold tight their dandelion heads.

                                    I continue.

Rain, too, is hostile. Breaks
on my face, goaded by wind.
                                        My clothes
are spared the launderette.
I resurrect the Brylcreem look.

                                    The streetname
dogpaddles into sight. 29,
28, (. . . the slushy rush
of my feet . . .) 27, 26,
. . . but where,
                    WHERE
                            is 25 . . . ?

Freedom

Finally,
nights without moon.
3 I've spent here
south of Séte
& no weak searchlight spoils the dark.
She's still fumbling among
the skypropping slums of London,
unaware of my departure.

But she's not unknown here.
Faint white footprints dot the sky,
& her Vichy collaborators—scorpions & mosquitoes—
ensure I do not sleep.

By day there is
sun. He has already begun
to scorch me. Will finish me off soon.

Perhaps I need moon here.
Her glow, bottled,
refrigerated,
would soothe the sunache, & she could
control her savage insects.

I will dispatch my pterodactyl
with a peace treaty.

Drought

Tap yields only dust
when wrung. Tea rots
in the cupboard. On radio
weathermen croak despair.
Too long in its hell, the Sahara
tires of loneliness.

                I stare
at sun. Today again at full-
power, grilling his
favourite planet for supper.
I wish he'd guzzle soon,
while we've still pain
                    as sauce.

Pale with embarrassment, moon
flits away the nights.
                    Won't dare
beg him for clemency.
Rain has suicided
                from uselessness.

I run at noon
            to lap my sweat
dry. Would sip piss if I could.

I've even tried my blood
                but sadly
there's no future there.

Nightlong

Jabbed by wind's spear,
        shadows prowl the wall.

I read to make sleep jealous.
The light dims with each word.
          Threatens to vanish
at the penultimate page.

Cliché conducts the music
                    I transistorise
to swap later for silence.

                    I try again.
Lightless I curl up, count
dodos diving to Atlantis.

But aches interrupt.
Worries tug my beard, &
enemies goad my memory.

And the curtain keeps flapping
aside, letting moon's footbeam through.

It won't be bedtime tales
            she'll come for, either.

Holland Park Walk

So early
that ghostdew dulls the grass.

Gates flex in their openness.
Trees & squirrels stare at me,
the lone intruder. I wish
tourists would hurry
& spread the humansmell.
My face feigns a faraway look.

Along poolgreen grass
to the peacocks.
What? Not there? The enclosure empty?
I send a wild glance
to prod bushes.
Scan clouds
lest they've rediscovered flying.

Not a feather flutters.
My morning is guillotined.

I slouch homewards.

A squawk brakes me. There,
free among the trees,
a peacock!
Strutting by, glaring at me.
2 more hurdle a fence
to join him.
I tiptoe off,
enter the flowergarden.

Oasis-serene. Colours Optrex my eyes.
Blooms smooth their petals for the day.

                                        And here too
I find them. Strolling through roses.
Lazing in the beds. 3 cronies
perch on the high wall,
                                             chatting.

Headhung, I leave,
                                        cursed
wrecker of the peacocks' leisure.

Deluge

Never before
          such unletup downpour!
Glass seems flimsy against this,
& as for the roof
                    (I inhabit
the nth floor flat, where
n + 1 = sky)
               —the splashing
basin is its biography.

Cars are speedboats notso-
far below. (The landed rain
creeps up the wall.) There,
now, is answer to their prayers!
A firmly drowned drought,
but rainchants can
               also be overdone.

(Rainwaves froth at shinlevel.
At least they'll reach here last.
At last an advantage
          for the stairy nth flat.)

But quickly, a galleon must be built.
Those chairs, presses, that
woodwormed table—they'll do.
A few spoons of muesli
& I'll hammer away till night.

And through the floodsodden
ceiling I'll sail,

(Noah II), guided
by the brightsilverylight-
ofthemoon.

‘I’m Dreaming of a White Xmas’

for Eamonn

Out there
                in the garden
among the weeds & the rusty cars
& the sodden sleeping grass
it stalks,

              —no,
not the shadow I locked outside,
not the ghost of Jack-the-Ripper
nor a Messerschmitt pilot
                downed in the Blitz,
none of those,
                      but come
quick & see.
Look at the moonglints
             on its rainsoaked antlers,
watch its tail
        propel it through the night
with thirst.
                  We’ll follow it,
step past the slobbered mouthfuls
of grass
            & march towards the midnight.

’Scuse me, can you tell us please
where it went?’ we ask &
—watching them hurry by—are
amazed at such unobservance.

But allalong we know,
& hammering on the pubdoor, we
demand entry.
                    Else we'll call the cops,
& they'd love to hear
                            of a reindeer
slurping Youngs' Special
                    to the chimes of midnight.

'Was Hast Du Mit Mond Getan?'

Vanished! My spyey
eyes have returned,
                tearfilled,
from thin air. Allnight-
long I slept & they
blinked and peered their way
through the tarred atoms of sky
& (apart from a wrecked sputnik
          & a few ghost spacemen)
nothing!
        Now, popping back
into my sleepdregged sockets,
                they vacuate.

'What have you done with moon?' I cry,
bubbling through my spittled toothpaste.
'You nightdredger, rockrobber, planet-
kidnapper, you!
              (whoever you are).
I suppose you've lashed her
        with a huge black lasso
to your backdoorknob,
                  & suspended her
above your weedy garden, (with a high
lead wall to keep her private.)
I hope you're happy now
      with your cratered balloon,
'cause I'm gonna get you!
                    My pterodactyl's
got her scent, & together
we'll flap to your rooftop.

Who's gonna save you then?

My advice is to volunteer
for the first trip to Venus!'

ZZZZ

Just
a little longer & it'll
all be easy.
(An old wise Aztec
told me once
that beyond a certain point
—marked by shimmering violet in the mind—
'you had it licked'.)

I swallow
the last black dregs.
Rock up the stereo volume
till the speakers bounce with pain.

Glued to the glasspane, moon
lullabies my eyes.
I turn away
& pinch my shadow hard. (Better that
than a scimitar on the sleeping skull,
a silencerclad luger
whistling through my teeth.)

No, we must be strong! Mentally
I solve a crosswordpuzzle
in medieval Mongolian.

Afterall, who else would
save my Klee reproductions
from thievery?
Locks?—Superthug could
sneeze them to smithereens!

Tomorrow
I'll enquire about a robot bodyguard,
an armourplated alligator.
But tonight
it's up to me. That must be dawn
waiting in the wings.
Just a little longer now. Just
a . . . . . .

1976

Ball

The pain oozes out,
out through the keyhole of this dark
room
        to prowl the empty terraces.
Tomorrow it will whoosh to the centrespot
& wriggle back inside me.
                        —An armourplated boot
& the bash begins. And I (ancestors: cow; southamerican
tree) have 44 feet, 4 fists, 22 heads (+ subs
& misc. ballboys) to entertain.—
                                Any wonder then
I dream in this shadowed shed? Of awaymatches
where the ground's a clifftop.
Where the nets stretch to let me free, & off
bounce, bounce
                over the edge
down to the blue, blue sea.

                        Escape?
Window's there for breaking. A few hops & .....
but I'm too studscarred & rainwarped now. Too attached
to the bounty-boots that hunt me.
And I could be worse off. (—Rugby for example.
At least I've had the perfect shape.)
And I'm on TV.
Yes, & there's the superannuation prospect
(—kids or pensioners, neither kick as hard).

Why this hissing then?

They might even play a benefit
                    for my services. . . .

Garden

Crammed in the chest of city
between the marshmallowfactory & the dogprison,
the punkrock recordstudio & the royal puttinggreen,
breathes a building.
Go there, & beneath 29 stories
                    find my flat.
Among the ivy is a bell—
dingaling it, & teapot in hand
I will rush to meet you;
bustle you inside, ripoff your coat,
play you fine floaty music
          to backdrop our excited chat.

The evening will rollerskate by,
& when, sadly, the lastbus revs,
you will tiptoe after me
out beneath the prehistoric moon
to meet my garden.

Look how it throbs with strength
—no roses, tulips, carnations or other pansies here—
just weeds. Grass, thistles, nettles
cacti, maneating-orchids—all palmtree high.
See how I've oozed them up—
wateringcan dawnduty, noon
fertilising feed (—excrement & sulphur only).
Care not to creep too close
—though they're but buds yet.

Tomorrow is a boom for bodyguards.
Soon I'll drag my home out here.

Dreams

Dreams are lies, you say;
are no lens aimed
        through tomorrow's gateway.
Dreams are swallowed laughter;
are fear's montage
flashed on the screen of dawn.

Waving Freud away
you sketch a scene: you
in a crowd, while nearby
a plane plummets down.
Didn't affect you, you say.
No, you watched the bulls,
bayonets on beef
        thudding towards you.
Up a tree you spidered
and who was there,
        dead,
wasn't it you?

Laughing, you drink the tea
        I've brought you
to fuel your rising.
Dreams?, you say—
breath has better use.
I pull the curtains,
        unleash the sunlight.
I read the morning paper:
Planecrash in Greece.
'Now where are the bulls . . . ?'

No Welcome

I'll close the door again.
No hugs or brandy-tots today,
no gossip even. Things have changed.

I mean it. Did you not see
the running men push past you
in the queued-up station?

Where are they going?—I haven't time
to spell the world in German,
or Morse either. It's late.

Take your foot away, I'm sorry.
Stop that taxi passing,
here's the tip. I'm still your friend.

Forgive me if my invite's bounced.
Blame the weather. Another time
when flies are free of fever

we can giggle, consume a crate
of beer with meat & mustard.
Today is different.

So go—don't ask where,
I'm human. But hurry.
And whistle as you leave.

Astronomy

It's not my birthday, & amnesties
are not acquired by prophets,
so I sit here on the seafront
in Aberystwyth, out of season.

This is my posting. Crowds
of shadows stand before me,
the perfect audience. And gulls,
waves. I can preach here.

Can stand on the band-pavilion
each midday, drone my news.
Hecklers are banished. I prefer that;
and applause always worried me.

Yet sometimes in the sea air I ponder
my despatch here—by cynics.
On a train; to stay here
till I invent laughter.

As if I fake the future!
No matter. I continue; my curved
telescope still functions . . .
Dark footsteps, growing.

Astronomy; that sharp star
is Venus, its clouds of gas.
I have seen through all.
I am excess.

The Statue

after Ritsos

Woken, we dressed
and followed the noise like magi
through narrow streets to the main square
where a fire fought the darkness
& around it a crowd sang.
Sleepyeyed, we stood there,
wine was thrust in our hands
then we too were singing.

The crowd grew, the flames probed the stars
and above the din a single voice soared
like a bull. Then we saw him,
young head high & laughing
flinging his clothes behind him
clambering up the statue.
And we suddenly knew his song:
of heroes & wild bristling horsemen
and now he was one. As proof
silence claimed him
and up there on that stone horse
stonewhite in the moonlight he sat
motionless. We all watched
as the noise seeped away,
then we slunk into the dark streets
from the dying fire and the statue
of two riders on the one horse,
stood for years in the square.

Dracula's Cathedral

After the snow & the long spring,
the black trees, black hills,
arctic lakes in summer heat,
boozy chatter by the campfire;
and the town, trams & towers,
fog, Dracula's cathedral.
—After this, what remains?
Pictures on hands of cards
dealt out by mildewed memory
to fill the years with,
and a note doodled
on the mind: 'It never happened.
Images from a book once stolen.
You forged that passport stamp.'

And what if it all was sharper?
What if when fog
swept down on Freiburg,
streets half-empty, you in black,
you'd shinned with a rope
up Dracula's cathedral,
stood on the spire there,
believed so much that you swooped,
a bat, out over blurs of houses.
That was it, remember,
that December night, after pizza & Chianti,
after the talk on mind & matter.
Photos?—Yes, here they are.
Pity the fog conceals.

The Birds

1.

The dead hour of insomnia.
Cats & the amplified clock.
Is there no end?

                                        Yet dawn
arrives unwanted, the calendar
unveils a lie.
                              So he tries again;
rolls over, a fakir, untrained.

Through the ghost-sound of pigeons,
the bin-men's commotion,
                              he can't give up.

2.

Once, in another climate
a boy gave up
                              at dawn's first stain
when, drawn to the window, he saw

hundreds of gulls & crows
line the yard
                              in offkey chorus
like a football-crowd
or a massacre mourning

and amazed, he got up,
went down the road
                                        past sleeping farmers,
played golf in the half-inch dew.

The Dentist

is an adept potholer
who pokes among the rocks
with a mirror and a steel point

and whose hands are strong enough
to prise two jaws open
and let his long needle

deep into the pink moss
that becomes a pink balloon
and floats off to tomorrow

leaving the rocks bare.
He flicks a switch; a drill
churns the rocks to dust

with a sound like a Stuka
as shrapnel flies, and the earth
shudders and moans.

He is hunting a place
to deposit gold, somewhere
dark and moist, private—

complaining he's
the rocks' friend
but never welcomed in there.

Music plays behind him
to mollify the earth
as he chats about the economy

and mixes some cement
to build up those rocks
better than before.

A Round House

Will somebody build me a round house
low on a headland. With thick walls
& shrunken windows, a view on all sides.
And an acre of sandy grass.

I will move there, like the birds in winter.
Unloading a trunk & domestic trophies,
then quickly a bucket of whitewash
while the dry wind lasts.

Fields away, the weather-station
will probe the sky.
Ships will cross in the distance
with goods for the city.

I will have rabbit-snares,
a boat for cod. And a high
fence for summer, its day trippers.
I will invest in a gun.

Holiday

Waking in a borrowed house
an Alsatian standing by the door
the sea a mile away swollen with rain
I raid the kitchen, assemble a breakfast.

Outside the gate creaks.
Fat crows are on the trees again
the bushes overgrown, spiders in the long grass
where last night's full moon went to ground.

I break wood & strike a fire,
watch the clock hands dither.
Today could bring visitors, the path empty
as the upturned boats on the beach since summer.

Meanwhile there is paper. I look around,
sketch improvements: blue lines on the walls
where a telephone flex should run
while the rain goes on with its dream of islands.

Blondbeard

Here at a snapped-off signpost
a man with a blond beard stands.
He has come a thousand kilometres
from München (or was it Wien?)
in a staggered & varied convoy
through sheets of French rain
anaemic bread & recycled beer
nights on the grass verge of autobahns
and the split-class ferry—
here to the apex of Ireland
where he can't get a lift.
Behind him, past a hedge
someone's rinsed knickers hang.
He stares towards Iceland,
sunk in the Atlantic, as cars pause
and roar back up the town.
His afternoon leans
to a mist of harsh sunlight
where millions of tiny mirrors
drift to a chewed shore.

The Monks

I look for bicycles outside the door
or a minibus with stickers for a convention
but all I glimpse is an old Volkswagen
good for burial in the nearby sea.
Yet nine monks are inside the pub
hogging a corner by the open fire
and apart from one snoring fisherman
have the barman's talents to themselves.

One rises, tall as a patriot's statue,
swirls his white rope to the jukebox,
buys the jagged sound of reggae.
A rough Latin leaks from their table.
I stand there on a parallel plane
unseen by them, drink my half-pint
and make for the first bend in the road –
a godforsaken place for hitchhiking.

Home

When I think of home I see
a white pebbledashed house
sharing a yard with an ex-dancehall
where Le Mans is taking place
with a pedal-jeep & tricycles, &
high on a wooden beam a boy sits,
a stopwatch in his hands;
and through a starred window comes
the fatigued sound of a tractor
stealing sand from the ocean
leaving a yellow trail on tar,
a choir of dog-yelps in the air.

The Return

When you return as if you had never left
what they will say to you will startle—
they who have grown towards walking-sticks
cut from local hillside briars, and
who have learnt rumours of your whereabouts
by heart, enough to flay the memory
of the boy once excellent at Latin
who never soiled his hands on village cattle

and who now stands there, amid boxes
carrying clothes of a future fashion,
back at the mat that once felt your tread,
as eyes find the paper in your pocket
and you know voices speak behind windows
but to you will say nothing, not ever.

A Goodbye to Germany, August 1978

The trees are walking, horseflies are out.
The rickety waltz of a candle flame
under the roof of the lookout tower
is taking two hundred years to die.

Wursts in the fire, crates of beer.
Voices, abused guitars. The dog Geronimo
barks at cars that brake in the dark
and empty a crew towards the smoke.

High in the Black Forest, a task for police
to sniff out the fumes of hashish
that lull Geronimo and float up the air
to that studious ghost in the tower.

Neighbourly Sounds

Awake to the neighbourly sound
of a woman reaching orgasm,
crying a name over & over
as if trying to sell his function
to all the street's women;
and her bed expands and contracts
till it feels like a battering ram
that has got my ceiling beaten
and I sit up in my bed
that's calm as an ice floe
a position that has become
a seat for a blind man
at a live sex-show; and just then
I notice dawn has come.

Rain

It seemed a good-sized lake fell
on roofs, tarmac & the odd tree.
All morning I heard the quick
intermittent hiss, aware that some
were being irrigated out there
rushing on, glum as punctures;
and that others were dancing
naked, to conjure just such rain.
And when it stopped there was
the quiet of rested saws
then birdsong came, and I felt
the shaking of soaked feathers
the taking again to the sky.
Its heights would now be dry.

Bad Blood

It's paint that's needed, that & nails
and a coachload of volunteers
who'd whistle and tell mighty jokes
and be done with all when the night's over.
Till then the calendar's damage remains.
I stand in the door and take count.
The curtains hang askew; light escapes
to the street to show there's someone here.
A full moon floats above the drainpipe
and a cat cries on an alp of junk.
And whispers begin to pierce the walls
from next door, from last year.
One step inside and already it's started—
bad blood throbs round a communal head.

The Window

There would be chairs there, at the window
like wagons, all in a ring.
For it's survival tactics. A lit fire,
certainly, & a pot of tea prepared.
And the net curtains kept black & dusty—
camouflage. No one must be seen.

Their number is unknown, small perhaps
as threatened species are. They speak little,
a background music plays on Radio 3.
Cars chug past at all hours.
Pens & notebooks would be somewhere
and nearby, a camera & telephone.

For years they have done this,
no strangers to blue strafe lights—
though the law is a sieve
with the holes worn large.
Portraits line the walls, a lineal row.
Night comes. Their duty is begun.

New Town

Arithmetic devised the town
and algebra fills it.
There are a hundred houses,
replicas of themselves,
and names are signed over
with the keys. Though newcomers
are rare, pale & quiet.

In a few days they know
the street's yardage,
its drains, lampposts,
the one willow tree
at the pond dead centre
where the square breaks out.
They walk easier now;

contribute to the laughter
as miniature paddle-boats
are sunk on the pond.
They nod and comment
as waist-high chessmen
are moved on the ground.
They get their chance too.

The cinema is gratis
though the same films return.
Meat is removed from recipes.
No one writes letters,
none are received
and no unplanned visits.
Yet life goes on,

a procession of numbers
smooth as the days,
and if a new cross sprouts
in the clay enclosure
then a train will come,
a man with a case
will emerge to a vacant name.

Lili Marlene

He sits at a table in artificial light
drawing circles on a page. A record
plays behind him, painting the air
the colour of old cleaned-up wars.

He thinks of the new strategies
that leave no room for blue fictions
only facts, such as radiation
& cockroaches who'll inherit the earth.

And stopped cars with their skeletons,
hotel suites, galleries, wine cellars,
music such as this—all for them
if they want. They possibly know.

The song begins again: words
about barracks, a corner light
and a girl who waits there at night.
He recalls a chemistry lesson—
how a tear makes a perfect meniscus.

A Fable

for Tim Dooley

It's there in the concave sky
clear as a poster.
Already the blueprint is underway.
And the people are hoarding their valuables
not banknotes, they won't last.

Leave that man on the makeshift coffin,
you know his speech.
OK he may have tapped the future
so what's to lose? Come here meanwhile
and see what I may see.

It's a roaring New Year party
at the century's end. Dispelling frontiers.
When trucks, still with wheels,
will bring the whisky.
And cows will roast at street corners.

Too far away! you shout,
Through miles of diary!
Remember Caesar. The date will come.
The babies born in 1980
will be twenty-one

And the bands they'll form
will shake the ancient houses.
A refined music in the sphere of rock.
Dancing, can't you feel it? Ah, no.
Call it a fable, then, and smile.

The Lake

Go there in winter, you will not find it.
You may take a train to Bärental as instructed,
emerge at a shop & a yellow postbox,
a farmhouse whose roof slopes to the ground.
Soon the forest begins—there is a path,
a sign saying: lake, x kilometres.
You will set off, your breath leaving
ghosts in the air. You will think it easy.

Snow is everywhere and the forest suits it.
You will have a map drawn by friends
showing fields with cows & other landmarks.
It would be perfect for autumn
but even now its navigational hopes are good
and helped by signposts it may
bring you close. Though you will be
least aware how close you are.

You will reach a small weir and be excited
at running water, though it is just a stream.
This is to be expected. And then
the path curves & begins to steepen
till above the white trees a hill rises
with skiers & a TV transmitter
& above this, clear sky. The lake
is beneath, you are almost there.

But still you cannot see it, though the map
is precise: *there* is the ridge
& *there* the Gasthaus, & the paths
winding up to the ski slopes.
By now light is dying. You give up
and return to the station, angry
at snow & trees that combine
to make ugly faces in the dusk.

You will return, of course, in summer.
This time you will find it, though not
with ease. Others will be there,
veteran adventurers, and you may
picnic with them, discuss the view.
Beer will be kept in the water
which is arctic, even now.
You will not mention last time.

Will lie there bare-chested by water
that was buried under snow.
It will all seem funny now,
the lake round & silver as a coin.
You will go to it & begin to wade
till someone shouts not to swim there,
that a whirlpool is waiting underwater.
It is true. I drowned there & remain.

Gifts

A man in a park avoids a boulder of snow
and hardly realises. He could be asleep,
a somnambulant nightwatchman.
Or a man choosing gifts for his wife.

He takes the memory of her that morning
and fits it out with gifts. Nothing suits.
Not gems—she has enough to fill a pyramid.
Not clothing either. And art is chancy.
It's four days to zero. What will do?

Perhaps he should know the park contains
many with this thought. Perhaps if they paused
beneath a tree and held a meeting, each
might help another and that way help himself.

Some, of course, get themselves as gifts—
silent versions, waiting in the blank
dressing rooms of new mirrors, among chairs
& blistered paint; and whose sleep each night
is a death where all records are erased.

New Year Party

I know your ways, older brother
and as the year ends I'll reveal them.
It's a good time for knowledge
an easy time for new pictures
even one as capsized as yours.

I adjust my tie, brush my suit
& organise the layout of the food.
You are on the phone this hour:
your laughter goes longdistance,
cheers up those who'll miss your party.

Half visible, I hover by the door.
Hundreds are expected. I hear the bell,
obey it—they rush to touch you
while I flit towards the stereo
to play your latest favoured band.

Coincidence, of course, has spoiled me
with that exclusive rear view
two years back in your cool slipstream.
And sometimes even I drew breath
in awe at your acting style.

But I stayed quiet, no one knew—
till this last stroke of midnight.
I have facts like a Nazi-hunter:
dates, letters, the odd photograph—
evidence stoked-up over years.

This night is asterisked a long time
and when I take the microphone
to list your New Year praise
I will watch your mouth collapse,
your smile freeze & fly at me.

The Servant

I am summoned: a double handclap
from my mother's ivory hands
and I fill the silver tureen
with pumpkin soup the colour of oranges.
I enter on feet of air.
Her smile subsides like a wave on sand
pointing me towards the curtain
of mauve velvet where I must stand.

Wine is shared. A toast to mother
updates a grace before meals
then the ladle becomes a wand
and oohs climb from warmed stomachs.
My timing is pre-set—
I conjure the plates away
to return, hidden by conversation,
with shark fillets in lime & butter.

I picture the absent fins & teeth
& a red dye in the sea.
Remove the bones, wheel in a trolley
on which a boar, freed from the spit,
sits in a juniper sauce.
Another wine now, old & crimson
then marble potatoes, celeriac matchsticks
& olive lentils puréed in butter.

I bring dessert, despite protests—
its exact identity mother's secret
though I smell figs & honey
in a foam the lightness of clouds.
Dispatched to the kitchen to grind coffee
I glance at the night through glass—
a slide where the stars are dandruff,
the moon a fingernail clipping.

Electric Nights

Sitting up halfway to dawn,
playing cards with the lights on fire
till the house must recall an ocean liner,
at times I ask myself
if daylight is real to them at all.
If they think the blue sky
an illusion, a backdrop to sleep
and strength for their electric nights.

I can't see them 500 years ago,
a family with an owl coat-of-arms,
staying frisky all night
to candles & live mandolin.
Last time I saw them was a party
thrown to prove they still existed.
I remember well the arc lights
arranged like guns around the walls.

It all began by accident,
a casual extra laze in the mornings
that progressed—may turn full circle
but watching them I doubt that.
Theirs is a night religion.
I get by on coffee now
and sleep later every night.
I hope soon to pass a dawn.

The Dancehall

Music jumps in the open window.
My feet fidget, test the boards, tap some
and I'm off out the door beyond the streetlight
to a dancehall built without my knowing.

Television has been ruining me.
I queue with strangers. Behind us
a bus with bald tyres empties.
I say: how will we all fit in?

At the door banknotes are requested.
Wrestlers in plainclothes stand & watch.
I pass and round the corner
to the first real blast of the band.

They are old & young, like a family.
A monkey in velvet by the drummer's elbow.
Floorboards have felt dreamier music.
The singer smiles & climbs his song.

And, my coat still on, I'm asked to dance
though how my feet know I can't say.
A girl with pink hair—I like her,
she grins like a puppet & speaks as much.

We whirr like windmills. The walls rock—
are we on a ship, in neutral waters?
There are all shapes of people here.
Fans like captive helicopters cool the air.

It’s Christmas. But what’s that din?
And shouting out of time with music?
That’s punching, and those are knives
glinting in the spotlights. That’s blood.

It’s not yours, I say, dance on
and I do but I’m tired.
I leave with a last look around.
I am the first one home.

The Ideal Home

The street should be curved
slow as the earth, and quiet—
a shortcut nowhere.

And, a dog's bark away,
a park—with pink birds
& imported foliage.

To find it should be map work
and no shrine should stand
to entice the tourist

so avoid the marks of fame—
those plaques that besiege
the door with cameras.

Better a small house
with a beard that cats climb
and that grows untrimmed.

And beyond this, some grass
where weeds grow discretely
and approach the gate.

The door, oak, of course
with many keys, and a hall
where the brute sleeps

and you, one floor above
on the swell of a waterbed
to his mantra snores.

The Hole

They came in early morning. I woke
to shovels & a jackhammer's pogo
& the cracks these antics left
in the car park across the street.
It was the first day of spring.

The view from my third floor eyrie
is angled, but spyglass clear.
Twenty times a day I stood there,
a coffee in my hand, and watched
the dig proceed in slow motion.

The dimensions were a tennis court's
sunk to a depth of six feet—
to the inside of a 30s' basement.
I saw the walls, the concrete floor,
the chimney, the ghost armchairs.

That was a week ago. Today
it's half full with sand & stones.
No chips of spines were found there.
Nothing was taken out, nothing put in
and it's almost flat again.

An invoice is out for cement.
Soon the black taxis will return
and nothing will remain of the hole
except this bored wonder I'll retain.
And the dreams I'll have of reasons.

A Crow's Cremation

We found him, beak to the light
on a sill in a locked-up room.
We had gone to admire the ceiling.
Laid him out on a stone step
while we discussed his demise—
how he blundered down the chimney,
that one-way passage, and how
he was beyond stink, feathers only.

His face was a black Apache's.
Eyes gone, the craters black too
and all of him stick-light.
We dropped him in the range
on blazing turf, and smelt smoke
beneath the roof, faint, then gone.

Mr Lu, the Guitarist

I was there when he first saw snow—
a whoop, or the flame in his face woke me
to see him standing at the window
in pyjamas with his clothes on underneath.
He wanted to barefoot it out there—
he with his allergy to English weather
who slept with an electric fire on all night
and enough blankets to leave him flat.

All his playing that day was offered
to the northern white that owned outside.
He wanted to stop the cars, the slushing feet;
left a glassful in the fridge
which I washed out a week later
while his fingers called Bach to the bedroom.
I told him as he hurried out
with his guitar to the windy, non-white cold.

The Obituarist

for Robert Greacen

Lives, these days, in a one-way street
next to a banjaxed launderette
with a Manx cat who jumps from sills
two floors up, and returns unmaimed.
All the world's jets pass overhead
whenever he sits down to tinkle Chopin.
And he's stuck with a crooked postman.
Each noon it's beef in oyster sauce
at the local Chinese, and a hunt
through reliable headlines in *The Times*.
His file of unfinished works includes
Böll, Reagan, Sinatra and the Pope . . .
Recovery affects him greatly, as does
a corpse catching him on the hop.
He once worked on a friend's notice
then brought tulips to the hospital.
They made a golfing date for June.
After he got home he made additions
inspired by a propped-up photograph
and a tumblerful of peaty malt.

The Infirmary

Was always warm and lit by personal lights,
a hideout from Caesar's Gallic Wars
or crosswords passed from desk to desk
while the prefect read Bond and listened.

The glass key was Matron's thermometer,
then the rare, schemed-for command
to kit out in dressing gown and slippers.
Supper was special from a dumb waiter
an hour early, in a hot aluminium hat.

No one was ever sick there, not visibly.
They came for Cup Finals or the Top Twenty,
played pontoon, spoke of mythical homes.
A flight of stairs away was the kitchen –
broached reserves of cold beef and cornflakes.

It was a room formed of infinite angles
four of which framed in the door,
and not even tongues warm from radiators
could stretch Matron's mercury all year.

Variation on a Dream

She dreamed it again, the death of her Mum
and Dad, in a city on the southern coast.
In this dream she missed the funeral—
dithered, drank, played table tennis
while her brother rang twice, in shock,
not seeing her eyes, her cheeks of chalk.

What were they doing there, in the one
city she thought of as cuddled by hills?
Why go hundreds of kilometres to die?
Last time all three had met was a town
north of the border, one brilliant Easter
when their squabble entertained a café.

Their deaths were separate, no accident—
that much remained. But stills of the dying
were cut, or dissolved in the daylight.
Now no one knew. A hotel foyer survived,
red petals on the doormat, a wet crowd
who turned and peered down the road.

In the dream, too, a car was outside—
on grass, the key in the ignition for hours.
The last earth was packed on the coffins.
The car door was open, someone was nagging.
Cows were heard next door, penned for milk.
She too was many kilometres from home . . .

Wild Garlic

Wherever it grew, it grows there still.
All I remember is a glass jar
and minute balls of brown, wild garlic.
They stayed out of sight in a cupboard
with boxes of letters and bric-à-brac,
to be eaten only by Grandpa and me.
He'd flick them to me across the table
after he peeled them with a fingernail.
I wish I knew that tart taste now,
our frequent alternative to sweets.

When he died, the jar stayed empty
and I never thought to ask directions
to where the garlic grew—
no survivor seemed to know.
It is years since I used his address
(his house with windows on the sea)
and though I'm told I cook like him
to recipes foreign and homemade,
and though my blood is garlic-thinned,
I've never chewed wild garlic since.

The Lame Waltzer

Crushed by an ambulance, he survived
to grow cacti for a living
and wear out tapes of Strauss.
We grew used to the lilt in the sea air
heard through holes in the wind,
to the limping shadow on the curtain
on the half-bright August nights
before the marquee pegged in town.

Together we traced his missing years—
his mail came from Germany, and once
a truck with Munich number plates
braked on the brae to ask me
where Herr Coyne, the cactus grower, lived.
Ah ja, I said, you want
the best lame waltzer in Europe,
and I aimed them at the tideline.

The Aerial

Because of a hill our TV snowed
even in August, on golfers, on elephants,
on supine girls sipping Cointreau.

If we'd bought a mile of cable,
lugged the aerial uphill, set it in a cairn,
faces might have been visible

but we thought of dynamite
or shifting the three storey house elsewhere
and did nothing but fight.

One day we reached the chimney
to counter the wind's adjustments, and swung
the aerial out over the sea

and almost fell when a shout
landed above—to lock the pole there,
come down to black and white.

We were friends for days
till an Atlantic storm took our picture
and good humour away.

The ladder came out again.
We aimed the aerial back at the hill,
recalled snow to our screen.

In time we forgot it
when we were at home—we learned to join
the facial or landscape dots

and kept the shotgun in trim
to obliterate gulls and greybacked crows
from the aerial's delicate limbs.

Heirs

In the country heirs are on the make—
out there in the fields, the sea nearby,
hedges, the circular wall of hills,
what better home for their campaign?
Streetlamps stop at the village edges
and if they stuff the collection-boxes
with paper, or are seen in company
with Germans who built a factory
bringing flocks of jobs to the parish,
what rancid adjectives can be applied?

But the gateposts and poles have eyes.
Late walkers get noticed, and drivers
who negotiate untarred lanes to
cottages and farms, their future plans.
The roof is already altered, almost,
and the sitting room extended.
Where was that Swedish shower advertised?
Meanwhile they bring bags of toffee
and sit in state on the best chair
within view of the antique, walnut clock.

Split-Level

A split-level bungalow has erupted
by the ruined parental home—
its walls are prison-modern,
its aerial nets Scottish TV,
its bay window magnifies the sea.
Portholes punctuate the corridor
past the main loo, to the garage
where doors open inside and out.
The site was a fairy mound, it's said,
before bulldozers or common sense.
Now a curly, tarmacked drive
stops at a gate, at the worn road.

Last week a tricycle sat out there
all night long, without theft.
It's gossip-evenings still—
at the bar the old boys relive
wakes in the adjacent ruin
when its thatch was rain-tight
and whiskey went down within,
and one, a mason, mutters
that six weeks would right it,
that the pair in the same grave
must be dizzy with turning,
that the bulldozer's due to return.

Sarsaparilla

Caravans in the marram by the 17th green—
this is where you'll find them on nights asleep,
six miles from the border in a European Mexico.

A flag and a proclamation, some photographs,
are tacked to the walls. Cars with foreign plates
graze outside, mud on their backs and tails.

The terrain ramps to the cliff of a quarry
where night-urinators would weigh up privacy
against freefall. These men piss in headlights

and gravity leads their porter under the traffic
to an arm of the ocean, where the lights
of a Soviet fishing ship are fixed as stars.

A song to a hero might waver on, twisting
into the dark, and a shot might follow,
liberating a puny avalanche of gravel—

though their firearms are mostly quiet,
kept for urban duty, those active nights
when their crouched figures move among graffiti

and others with the same tattoos lean on the bar.
Or perhaps the same veterans, a little early,
checking their watches, sticking to sarsaparilla.

The Night Post

All night the filaments stayed red
courtesy of the nation, and I wore
wool beneath my tunic and smoked
while Grant sucked mints the loud way.
We'd each made coffee, I remember,
and I'd waved a whiskey-smuggler through
after receiving a sample, and Grant
had turned a Morris Minor inside out,
hunting in vain for a similar cargo—
when the Mercedes hearse came along.

It was 3 a.m. or thereabouts, a moonless
sky, and the driver wore a top hat.
Was as courteous as any ambassador.
I moved my beam down the long box
trying to picture the bloodless face—
was a beard still growing there, or
did it breathe, indeed, eyes on the lid,
or were there dozens of Armalites?
I bid the man a gruff goodnight,
walked in, envying his Brando face.

The Shark

Was two ton at the end of the line
or on the trailer towed through town.
How they heaved him up escapes me,
those Englishmen, there with their boat
for a fortnight in salmon territory.

They had oysters with Guinness, as word
whizzed through the town's pubs
till we all emerged holding glasses,
prodding the black sides, pulling
those lips back to gaze at the teeth.

I earned free chow mein by a call
to the Won Pagoda, and Xieng himself
braked his Ford in the muck, eyeing
the geometrical fins jagging the air
which he alone measured for saucepans.

And I oversaw the dismemberment—
the off-white chunks hung on hooks
in Granddaddy's coolroom, the head
alongside, at the end, like a signature
that I showed the kids at 10p a go.

Geometry

When I sold my setsquare and protractor
and Euclid's Collected Theorems
I knew I had abandoned geometry.
What use was a science of shapes
in a world of miniskirts?
I bought some daffodils instead.

Coins and walls were still around
and the long curves of thigh.
I took up mediation –
in time I'd lose this college vision.
I hitchhiked to the hazy air
of all the dens in Europe.

Call it the geometry continent!
Every town was bulging with it –
Mondrian, Gaudi, Eiffel's pole.
In Holland I woke in a square field
where parallel lines of motorway
stretched to that final cube of clay.

The Mugging

That night I was mugged twice in a dream
on Leather Lane and Gray's Inn Road,
annulling my late-night poker earnings.

I woke remembering tears on the step
as I'd turned the key, and thought it true.

As once, pissed on Cuban rum, I dreamt
I'd lost one of my only shoes, and felt
beneath the bed to find the dream true.

This time, despite the Cheapside hotel,
the muggers' words, the dream-borders held.

Five played cards at an upstairs table,
among them a hall-of-mirrors distant friend,
then I walked away with forty quid.

The first boys were amiable, even joked
as I fobbed them off with a fiver each.

The second lot went through my pockets,
kicked me, left me with my clothes.
I recognized no one in either crowd.

The light from the lamppost showed rain
as their steps echoed through empty streets.

The Pitch

The goals are crooked on the snowy pitch
but errant shots won't score today,
won't kindle a school-burning controversy.
And no one sleeps on the centre circle
in an orange tent, refusing to leave,
reminding the Head through a zipped door
that the lunches are execrable, the loos
public, the everyday laws childish.
The muffled reporter (and one-time student)
won't find a story here, not unless
she imagines well and wields a grudge
and she's much too ambitious for that.
A mouse lies stiff in the penalty area,
smoke shadows the perimeter trees,
footprints traverse the piebald surface
on the shortcut to the go-slow trains.

A Holborn Lamppost

I'm halfway down a Holborn lamppost
with the warm bulb in my hand.
I'm barefoot for the chimpanzee grip.
Imagine a warm night in October,
a couple of quarts of special bitter
then the mischievous gambol home.
My bushy cousin is on the pavement—
an accomplice, a lookout is needed.
A big boy, he is fair at rugby
and a rare hand at the double-bass.
I'm stationary, taking a breather,
considering the lure of Tandoori smells.
My cousin raises his whisper, points
to the corner where a cop is hiding,
peeking round, blue hat in his hand.
He's like that, my Yorkshire cousin.
A plane whines above me, heading west.
I'm twenty tomorrow, at 3 a.m.,
and finally I've a head for heights.
But perhaps it's time I slid down.

In the White City

The underground telephones are free
though you can queue for hours,
grabbing pies from the vendor
who rollerskates by, and rain
is spectacular as fireworks,
and the toffee shops are domed
and everyone owns a wolf
and once a morning a voice,
liquid and chilled, leaks from speakers
high on the lampposts, enquiring
about our health, about the babies,
about the taste of the new icecream,
and skeletons of the presidents
sit in marble chairs in the park
that leads to parliament, the grass
delicate as smoke, the police
in cloaks and wooden sandals,
and everywhere, the oddest smell
of mangoes or pawpaws, mixed
with the burning of seaweed.

Divers At The Laurentic

The divers have left the Laurentic
to the crabs and flatfish.
Already they're past Malin Head.

And now they'll veer South,
along the East coast, or West,
until Ireland disappears.

For three weeks their dredger
sat in our bay, while they
felt around in the wreck

that settled there in 1917,
courtesy of a German mine
or a snorkelling U-boat.

They know they're not original.
They have predecessors
who, forty years before,

broached the Laurentic's cargo
of gold bars
to the tune of five million.

They know a sixth remained
and it's now on the move
under their unknown flag

while at a wake, on land,
men spend the night
talking about sunken gold.

The Cold

After the all-hours drinking bout,
and the punchless acrimony,
he set off for the sea, on foot,
a good mile in the wind,
past zigzag lines of parked cars
and the disco din, past streetlights,
though if he'd needed light
the stars would have done—
down to the beach he wobbled,
a beer can in both pockets,
to sit on a rock and drink,
and think of his marriage,
and when both cans were empty
he removed his shoes
to walk unsteadily into the sea
and make for Iceland,
but the Atlantic sent him home again,
not a corpse, not a ghost,
to waken his wife
and complain of the cold.

The Sea At Pollan

Annie Denny
who lived in the house above the sea,
a scant half-mile down from me,
could read the clouds
and predict a drowning,

not that there were many
though once when I was six or seven
a procession of men and women
snaked uphill—
I saw it from my room

and at its head
four men carried on an old door
a brother they'd lost a week before
who'd bobbed to land
at the base of a cliff,

the same cliff
pups and kittens were thrown from,
there being no way home—
except when a door
was lowered on ropes.

From the top
on a blue morning you can see Scotland
and pick the best mushrooms in Ireland,
then hit the road
at Annie's house

though she's long gone
and the barbed wire guarding the field
is now loose enough to yield
when you climb over
with a bag of mushrooms.

Down the road
come German campers in twos and threes
to their orange tents by the sea
on the ex-golf course
that earlier still

in neutral days
saw a Messerschmitt forced to land
by its empty tank, and farmers surround
it with pitchforks
till the army came.

It's quieter now
in Pollan. At night the cars come
and sit there with their radios on
at a country station
that's good for love

and one night
a friend and I crept, cursing, past
carrying between us a baby bath
three-quarters filled
with the sea,

fronds and all,
in a beer-inspired attempt to keep
two lobsters alive—we'd bought cheap
from a fisherman
after we'd eaten.

Dog On A Chain

This red setter was another red setter
who ran with his red tongue out
down the road, over fields and sand
into the sea; who came out shaking water
and loped by himself the long way home,
then lay on pebbles in the sun.
But after the car from over the border
mashed his hip, he lay on a rug
then limped for years, till a lump
grew on him, and the vet brought a gun.

In this second life he is lithe again
and doesn't howl at the chapel bell.
He howls at his long chain instead
that keeps him from the car-filled road,
and from the sheep and cattle
and their farmers who threaten guns.
But the next time he slips the chain
he'll run with his red tongue out
down the road, over fields and sand
into the freezing, gull-cluttered sea.

The Border

Twenty miles south is the North
where I was booked in to be born –
a nursing home in a Derry suburb,
but my mother went on playing bridge
and never made it past the border.

Fireworks, coconuts and kippers
came over later, and stones of butter
packed under the Volks's back seat,
away from the confiscating urge
of the Customs man in his warm hut.

It wasn't butter the B Specials wanted
when their bullets skimmed our bumper –
we'd missed their waved red light,
so shouts interrogated us
while a torch beam frisked the car.

These nights headlights go off
as you cross the border, and rifles
in soldiers' hands motion you to stop
outside the sandbagged checkpoint
that gave some local mason work.

Digesting Crab Claws

'Don't fall apart on me tonight . . .'
The tape's up loud and Dylan's back
from the Crusades, and we sit
half a mile from the frothed Atlantic,
digesting a bucket of crab claws
as the sea wind tests the putty.
An hour now and we haven't stirred
from this table, except to change
the tape, and feed the range
that eats turf like a generator
though its back boiler is holed.
And I pulled on the anorak
to go for turf, past the line
where a blue flag of jeans
makes the pegs earn their keep,
and back inside, I spoke
of slates that scythed down,
and of snapped-off branches.
No one listened. They stared out
at the would-be mountain opposite,
as if someone scuttled there
wearing red, past the houses,
then their upwardly errant sheep,
to stand, hunched, on the ridge
with the cairn and the TV booster
barely visible to us below.

The Crab Rock

Even in a bad summer the tide goes out
till the crab rock is revealed,
though the crabs like sun, like to climb there
and lie, as if dead, or lazily scuttle
among themselves, over weed and mussels.

Enough of their dead litter the beach
on the approach to the rock, waiting for water
to move them, out where no dog
or gull can poke them, where they'll dissolve.
They are back before the others know it.

The crab rock is never embedded in sand,
always those yards for us to wade through,
then the walk through edible claws
on bare edible toes. There are many crabs,
they are home, they are armoured.

I bet they leave when the sea covers,
though it's seldom deep there. A man could stand
all night and keep his head in air.
There are worse pastimes. Rain wouldn't matter.
The crabs would keep their distance.

The Lighthouse Keeper's Son

got arrested
as he wobbled home
on a lightless bicycle
after a late drink,
and he asked the cop
if the pockmarked moon
wasn't light enough
not to mention the Plough's
seven stars,
and his dad's beam
igniting the road
twice a minute,
then searching the sea
the umpteenth time
for nothing

Calais

Even the playground is empty,
the sun polishing the yellow and blue
of the domed climbing frame,
taxis and cars parked at home—
perhaps it's a day for Calais,
leaving by coach early,
the hovercraft, the seasick,
the late, clinking arrival back.

But who's this back so soon,
wheeling her case alone
up the concrete path, waiting
at the lift door, stretching
her back, till she disappears
up to whichever floor
her empty flat is on?
How long has she been gone?

Weeks, at least, I'd say.
Perhaps she'd meant to stay
a lifetime, but relented—
and now, dutyfree-scented,
she unpacks, undresses
while the shower hisses
to the right temperature,
and in the ghosting mirror

she glimpses her face
that's older than the face
he remembers, but kinder too,
ready to have a go
at loving him again,
hoping he feels the same,
then she soaps the sweat away,
and the dust from here to Calais.

Boy With A Rod

Along the bank of a river,
past resting swans,
a boy with a rod is running—
he must be fifteen
and the rod must be fifteen feet,
and the line and hook
are switching the air,
scarcely avoiding branches,
scattering oncomers,
till, with a laugh, he reaches
his stationary friend
whose hook waits in the water.

And, watching from the patio
of a still-empty pub,
between sips of ale,
a new-to-each-other
man and woman see
the boy flick his line
till it half-disappears,
and settle his boots
to wait all evening,
then perhaps let the fish go—
just as the man and woman
may never meet again.

Hitchhiking

The role of sex is exaggerated –
though a blonde at a motorway slip road
will jump the queue. Best to pair off,
then hide while she thumbs alone.
Watch for knives beneath the dashboard
and sullen men. Jeeps are alright,
especially if a map of the world
adorns the bonnet, and the driver says
he's back from a three-year trip
round the globe, and he takes you
on a tour of the Mâcon villages
to sample the wines, then home
to his château and Maman, and a bed.
Take care to keep awake in cars,
otherwise you'll double back
100 kilometres, cursing your Italian,
and at night, on the French border,
get in with a Yugoslav, bound for Paris
but crazy with the toothache,
who asks if you're a dentist,
then swigs his Slivovitch again.
It helps to have French ancestors
and enough of the lingo to relay this.
It helps to be an actor, and carry
a red towel for bullfight towns,
and a thick felt-tip for signs
on the backs of maps, names of cities
you've read about, and '1 kilometre'
for occasions you're stuck.
Watch out for Frankfurt cops
who shunt you on the autobahn,

then book you for the privilege,
and you're stranded there till a kid
shows a red breakdown triangle,
then beckons you to run.
Be prepared to climb into anything
from a Daimler to a knacker's truck
whose stench makes you puke
and sends kids scurrying in towns.
Draw the line, perhaps, at a hearse.

Leaving The Surface

Consider it probable
that today, on some blue-skied atoll,
a team of men are busy,
naked to the waist, and sweaty,
lowering bundles
of Perspex and fibreglass
to frogmen builders,
at it for years,
constructing a fabulous city
no satellite will see,
whose handpicked, future citizens
watch no screens
nor read no papers—
they include brewers and bakers
but no military—
already they can see
the identikit homes
they'll dive to when the call comes,
leaving for looters
address books and furniture,
leaving bills unpaid,
abandoning their dead,
keeping only the heat
from the piped, filtered sunlight,
leaving the surface
to its own devices.

Dredging The Lake

While it rained they dredged the lake again.
There was no one about, no one watching—
that was what they thought. They were wrong.
They thought they were safe, mid-morning
before term began, in a sea-fall of rain.
They forgot there are folk who don't belong.

They had one hour, with a boat and a van
with a winch on top. They worked fast—
five of them, all men with hoods up
and waders to the crotch. Pros to the last,
they hunted for something—a drowned pup,
the bloated, eyeless body of a man?

Whatever it was they bumped off without it
over grass, with the boat winched high—
though they did bunch together, I recall,
at the water's edge. Or do I trust an eye
that the rain kept indoors, and that later lit
on a jogger in red who kept it in thrall?

The Statues

I stared through the bay window
past a fly sunning itself
as it listened to birdsong.
On the left, a long-jump away,
stood a magnolia in flower,
shedding its leaves in May.
On the right, a pink rhododendron
was being cased by a bee
while ahead, in the shelter
of a medieval larch,
in a diminutive sentry-box
stood Joseph and the Infant
amid an audience of bushes.
I stared past the greenhouse
and the heaped pots of paint.
Behind me were thirty doors
(if you count the dumb waiter),
all in this small house,
some opening nowhere,
some showing ex-classrooms
with the desks intact,
awaiting exams; some locked
or ushering one into armchairs
arranged in a ring
next door to the kitchen –
and everywhere, statues
watching over nobody
in those rooms, those corridors,
Mary, the Boy, the Man,
the Saints and the Blesseds,
conspiring in an almost-whisper

to remind of the decades
where nuns' skirts were long
and there were queues to fill them.

The Haunt Of The Night-Owl

At midnight the hum of the telly goes on
when the voices are abed. I hear it
from my bed, one floor above, till you
shuffle over to fiddle the knobs, hoping
for other voices, anything still awake.
Your favourites are snooker and crime
but tonight you switch off, and your voice
slips through my floor like a gruff ghost,
waking the old woman on the mattress
next to yours in that mess of a room
where the radiators stay on in summer
ever since your TB, her diabetes,
and where the windows stay closed.
All night you mutter about nothing,
and none of it good, making sure
she hears you (you reach me too . . .),
breaking out into roars, sometimes,
when she shits, then rolls, in the bed.
You're not one for baths, much, yourself.
I can sniff when you've been downstairs
with your two carrier bags for basics—
bread, milk, clanking bottles of beer;
to answer the door or handle our mail.
Each morning a black nurse visits—
how this bugs you, but nowadays
you admit her, you've been warned
and you're getting on—and twice weekly
an ambulance cools outside, as two men
carry your woman down in a wheelchair
and away, to return her in hours.

Often when they get here, you're out,
or asleep, grabbing rest for the night.

Omelettes

A mattress stands on its side
with a cat asleep on top.
Behind it, the musty curtains
admit a chunk of sunlight,
while before it, a man of 70
lies, in his clothes, in a bed
and waits for the ambulance.
A tin with roll-up butts,
two cups, and a Pils can
are on the floor; the smell
is of urine and damp wallpaper.
He complains of the pain
in his bandaged arm and knee.
and talks to the other bed
whose owner now is dead,
two weeks back, and looks
at me. He speaks of the hospital,
how he knows the area well—
how he lived and worked there,
a second chef in a defunct hotel,
eight years, and he asks me
how many omelettes there are,
then answers, hundreds,
and tells me the best he saw
was when he took treacle
in place of oil, and the first chef
got the omelette off intact
and he doesn't know how he did.

No Answer

A woman in curlers sits by a phone,
a blue phone to a white house.
All morning while the friseur pattered
she catalogued her phrases
but all morning the big chief was out.
She has so much to tell him –
about poverty-deterrents, juggled figures,
a tax that's a new contraceptive –
that an airlift might be called for,
a Harrier from the South Atlantic,
taking off and landing in the dark.
She pushbuttons again: an empty ring,
where can the guy be? The friseur
is back to liberate the tresses
she will flaunt at a flashlit lunch,
after the microphones and biros
and the midge-drone of their owners.
She swallows; why are kippers bony
in this nuclear age, and why does
tannin not dissolve the bones away?
A mirror tours her head
till dismissed by a nod. It'll do.
She connects, then hangs up again.
The damn fool is never home.
Spends his life making dates
with bald, hatted men, on icebergs.
Why don't they meet on the moon?

How Witches Went Invisible

They boiled a black cat alive,
boiled it till the bones loosened,
took these singly in their teeth,
then stood before a mirror
till one bone defied reflection.

With this they were grinning winds
whooshing through the alleys,
masturbating in the marketplaces,
making pigs' heads float,
heading for home with fresh roots
and black cats at their see-through feet.

The Queue

At dusk I took a double-decker to the queue
that I knew would be there already.
I brought with me my sleeping bag—
it was a warm evening—also a book,
salt beef on rye, a naggin of whisky,
and my walkman primed with Tom Waits.

I know not everyone likes Tom Waits
but I do. I was right about the queue
(one extra reason for the whisky!)—
there must have been up to twenty already.
I unrolled my sleeping bag
and wriggled in, then opened up my book.

I suppose I should tell you about that book.
It's one of my favourites: *The Weight*
of a Corpse is Varied. The sleeping bag
was duck-down and the best in the queue
that had grown behind me already.
I took a shuddery swig from the whisky.

Would I, I thought, be mugged for my whisky?
Perhaps I'd brought the wrong choice of book
when thoughts like this already
were in my head. We had a long wait
till 9 a.m., and with this size of queue,
might end up with nothing. As sleep in a bag

goes I had a good night in that sleeping bag.
I slept for an hour at least. The whisky
lasted well. I was the envy of the queue
as I slid it to my lips, behind the book,
with the crackly seepage of Tom Waits
in the street-lit air. Then it was dawn already

and I watched my queue-mates all ready
themselves—some left their sleeping-bags
to walk around, forgetting the wait
they still had. I finished the whisky
and lay on, chortling at my book,
by this stage in the vanguard of the queue.

You must be wondering about this queue.
If I said each of you would be ready
to join it, with or without a book,
(most had none, though they had sleeping bags)
you'd say I was too long on the whisky,
like that stubbled croaker, Tom Waits.

But I'll say more. I'll say this queue's for books,
for sleeping bags, for tapes of Tom Waits,
for whisky, for anything, and you're in it already.

Her Song

Singing, she pedalled over the moonlit bridge.
Did the trout in the river listen
to her alto warble, or did the words
go unheard to the lowest stars?
Her own words, wedded impromptu
to the theme tune from *Doctor Zhivago*—
words that detectives in bushes
would relish, but they were still in bed.

And already behind her, the moon was outdone
by the flames in the thatch, showing
the whitewash going brown, then black,
the pony rearing at his rope,
the Saab locked in the yard,
and no one in burning pyjamas
framed for a second in the doorway.
Her song was telling the trout why.

The Coffin Shop

In the coffin shop everyone is busy,
there are three hands at every phone.
They still approach if you're in a hurry
—they recognise the recently alone,
and drop the chatter to be beside you
in white suits, with mauve bow-ties.
Their eyes are expressive as pandas
who have mastered maths. Their talk
swings to holidays in the country
where the corpse is headed, at expense,
a detail they arrange, while you look
the coffins over, to their commentary
of how each was made, and the lead
that lines this one, to deter invaders,
and the gold on that one, and the wood.
They poke the velvet cushions for the head,
they stand back and turn to face you
—you'd hardly decline if you could.

A Diary Of Symptoms

For weeks I've kept a diary of my symptoms
for my eyes alone. It lies in the drawer
with the carbon and the blank paper, as if
it belonged there. I keep the poems apart.
At any waking time I bring it out
and add the latest news from the body.

I'm trying to be helpful to my doctors.
I'll show them I, too, am professional,
and maybe we'll win. I don't demand much—
just health. I'm not hunting my youth
or a sprinter's fitness, or a priest's looks.
I just want to be here to write some books.

The Stone Ship

The stone ship sailed with a skeleton crew,
none of whom knew what to do.
And twice each day a postman left
with a red bag of mail, and a white.
And three canaries sang upstairs,
and once a policeman came and warned
the trusting, underpaid crew.
They still didn't know what to do.
Their bar in the hold was rarely open
and when it was it was empty.
No neon lettering lit up their door,
no one knew they were there
except for a batty few
who tried to tell them what to do.
They hated their twelve telephones
that never once stopped ringing.
The last remark of Marco Polo
would be a typical query,
and faced with this dialling queue
none of them knew what to do.
Some sat for hours in computer light,
some wrote letters to the bank.
Occasionally, one would paint the stairs
or change the wine in the bar.
There was so very little that was new,
little that was right to do.
The dusty directors kept away,
unless they met on the pier
to talk among themselves for an hour
and vote for each other in turn,
then shout directions at the crew.

They knew even less what to do.
So the stone ship sailed out of view.

Torchlight

Listen, the squeak of sandals on parquet floor,
the swish of a monk's brown habit . . .
It's Bob again, Bob of the biceps, Bob
who'll heave boys out of bed and slap them,
in the sudden daze of torchlight,
and make a date for the morning.

Whispers down the dorm link Bob
with the young nun in the sick bay,
the one I stare at, go there to see.
Soon she'll leave, I know that—
I half know why. It's there in
The Italian Girl I read under the bedclothes.

It's there, or I force it there,
then lie in the dark, thinking,
while whispers precede an ambush,
perhaps for me, that'll mean squeals
and scuffles, and the prefect's arrival
with his torch-beam bouncing off the floor.

Singing

Singing never pleased his grandma.
It sent her up the apple tree
to howl, and she was big,
a danger to the bottom branch.
What was it about singing
that bugged her? Her ears
could cope with shouting, easy,
but put a tune in there,
sit it on the surest voice,
and she'd be out, and up the tree.
The cat used to stare at her.
The grandson rattled coins
and contemplated genes.
He quizzed her about affairs
with tenors, in the 20s.
He took up the guitar,
wrote bad songs, and practised
in the disused toilet
at the top of the garden.
His voice attracted gulls.
He did the odd shit while up there,
for old times' sake. On days
when the wind was from the North
shreds of his songs reached the kitchen
and his pot-stirring grandma.
He'd have to coax her down
while the stew burned.

The Hill

After the visitors and their children,
after the rearlights have vanished,
I go inside to stare out at the hill
that fills my window, and I remember
climbing there with a Christian Brother—
I must have been ten—and sitting
by the cairn on top for an hour or more,
speaking little, watching the toy cars
move between villages, and the birds—
we had a dog with us, a black cocker,
who barked them away—come hovering close,
and I should have gone back there
when the house was full of shouts
and simmerings, but it's quiet now
in every room, and I go upstairs
to stare out at the sea instead, past
a flurry of starlings, heading somewhere.

The Knowing Birds

A gull laughed at me,
laughed three times and flew on,
and the smell of dried blood
rose from the green
and followed me on the wind.
There was no escape
in the sandstone, no caves
to hide in, and the sea
was stormy, the beach boat-free.
I caught a magpie
with the side of my eye, heading
towards the house
where a family of swifts
sat on the wires
outside my window, and saw
right through me
day after day, and the baby
flew in once, and turned
in the trapped air
above me, then flew back out.
Why would it stay there?

Whatever

What does he think, this man
in the hospital bed, knowing
he's dying because he heard
she was sleeping with a neighbour—
perhaps she taunted him
until he grabbed the bottle
of weedkiller, and swallowed,
and now his kidneys are dead,
dead as he'll be soon?

And what does she think, knowing
she called in the other man
who, showing it was harmless,
swallowed weedkiller too—
and he's in another hospital,
fighting to live, and the whole
town is talking about her
and her two kids, and all
because of sex, love or whatever?

Breaches

for Irmgard Maassen

Glühwein with honey at Potsdamer Platz,
at the breach that drew the biggest cheer
when the pastel-coloured Trabis drove through.
Slush underfoot, wrecking shoes.
In the darkening distance: the Reichstag.

As we approached the Wall, we heard
a deepening tapping, a chipping that spread
till it was everywhere. Then we saw them:
men and women with mason's hammers and chisels,
and bags on the ground; two Frenchmen
attacking the parapet, making sure
nothing fell on the East; cracks that widened
to let blue-uniformed *Volkspolizei* peep through,
as they paused in their paired stroll,
while on the West, two cops in green
walked up and down, with megaphones,
advising the chippies to leave the Wall alone,
at once, or else . . . or else . . .

We took our tiny hammer and whacked chips
from that graffiti-daubed, astoundingly thin,
infamous construction, helping in our way
to make it disappear.

NOVEMBER 1989

Blue Eggs

The hens that laid the blue eggs
were Lavender Araucanas
and came from Chile, and the blue
(a darker blue than ducks' eggs)
got inside the shell as well,
and the eggs tasted better,
or so her friend said, proudly,
to people who'd never heard
of blue eggs, and who frisked
the friend for traces of a joke,
then finding none, asked
how they'd buy blue eggs,
how they'd contact her. But she
was on a farm somewhere, incognito
as any ex-teacher—and who
wouldn't be an *ex*-teacher
in these National Curriculum days
when they could box blue eggs?

Bears

for Nicholas Jardine

Someone is sending me bears—
bear cards, teddybear cards,
I've had three so far.
'Apologies for bear militant'
introduced the last one,
and the bear was a German,
dressed as a sailor
in the First World War.
All the bears were German,
from the pensive first
through the pugnacious second
to the militant third.
And the handwriting is familiar
but forgotten—who is this
bear-man, or bear-woman,
and where will it end?
1920 is the latest date.
The soles of this bear's feet
are leather, and his eyes
are glass. His long nose
juts out over his collar.
The sewn-on red anchor
on his blue-serged arm
points to a paw in a cuff.
What will the next one wear?
When will enough be enough?

The Dark

There were owls in the moonlight
as we cleared the mountain—
such high fliers, such safe voles
in the fields underneath.
Then we swung out to sea
and back in, over the headland
with its ruined castle,
its football pitch, its cave.

Someone had kindly
lit bonfires on the touchlines,
but the pitch sloped
and the wheels threw up mud.
I managed to stop
in front of the goalposts,
and we took our sleeping bag
to the dark of the cave.

Banknotes

A room empty except for banknotes
scattered on floorboards, and curtains
to keep this secret—and who
sent her the key and the address?
She had these four weeks before
she used them, begrudging the fare,
trudging through rain to a house
so dingy she tried to turn away.

But she'd travelled an hour, and the key
showed her the banknotes, like litter—
like leaves, as they were tenners
and inches deep. And watermarked, too,
in the torchlight. And when her bag
was bloated, she filled her clothes,
every item, then rustled to the door
she locked, holding onto the key.

The Flying Spring Onion

The flying spring onion
  flew through the air
    over to where
the tomatoes grew in rows
  and he said to those
    seed-filled creatures
My rooted days are done,
  so while you sit here
    sucking sun
I'll be away and gone,
    to Greenland
  where they eat no green
    and I won't be seen
in a salad bowl with you,
  stung by lemon,
    greased by oil,
and nothing at all to do
  except wait to be eaten.
With that he twirled
  his green propellers
and rose above the rows
  of red balls
who stared as he grew small
  and disappeared.

Fishbones Dreaming

Fishbones lay in the smelly bin.
He was a head, a backbone and a tail.
Soon the cats would be in for him.

He didn't like to be this way.
He shut his eyes and dreamed back.

Back to when he was fat, and hot on a plate.
Beside green beans, with lemon juice
squeezed on him. And a man with a knife
and fork raised, about to eat him.

He didn't like to be this way.
He shut his eyes and dreamed back.

Back to when he was frozen in the freezer.
With lamb cutlets and minced beef and prawns.
Three months he was in there.

He didn't like to be this way.
He shut his eyes and dreamed back.

Back to when he was squirming in a net,
with thousands of other fish, on the deck
of a boat. And the rain falling
wasn't wet enough to breathe in.

He didn't like to be this way.
He shut his eyes and dreamed back.

Back to when he was darting through the sea,
past crabs and jellyfish, and others
like himself. Or surfacing to jump for flies
and feel the sun on his face.

He liked to be this way.
He dreamed hard to try and stay there.

Johnjoe's Snowman

Johnjoe built a snowman
shaped like a wigwam
and postbox-sized.

What he didn't tell
was that inside the snowman
he'd stuffed the cat.

All Sunday morning
he patted with his shovel
the sides of that snowman.

He didn't bother with a head.
He'd never seen a snowman
that looked real yet.

How was it a snowman?
Because Johnjoe said so,
and he should know.

When it was finished
he stared at the snowman
and saw it wasn't right.

What the world didn't need
(apart from frozen cats)
was another white snowman.

In memory of the cat
he took the snowman
and sprayed it black.

Night Boy

After the cat went out
and the moon sat on the hill
and the sea drowned a lorry
that broke down
                    stealing sand,
little, skinny George awoke.

He was little, because he hardly grew.
He hardly grew, because he ate
scraps of chicken, leftover rice, dry bread,
what was left on the dog's plate,
handfuls of cornflakes, jam.
That may sound a lot
but it left George little and skinny.

What about mealtimes? I hear you ask.
Mealtimes, for George, were sleeptimes
most of the year. That's right,
he slept all day,
                    got up at night.

What about school? you're saying.
I know, I know what you're like.
What do you know about stars?
Does the sea glow at night
like a green watch dial?
Ask George, he'll tell you.
He'll even write it down
and read it to you, by torchlight,
and then he'll count the stars.

Blame the holidays, his Gran said,
they're too long.
George lived with his Gran,
George, the sleeper-in
who'd slept in so long, so often,
that now he woke at night
when Gran was asleep.

What did he do at night?
He went to the beach,
lit driftwood fires,
stood in a cave and waited
for spies in submarines
to land.
          He climbed hills
and aeroplane-spotted,
especially small ones
landing in fields.

He hid in ditches
and eavesdropped on strangers.
He woke the neighbour's donkey
and galloped round the field.

He lay on a haystack
and watched the dawn.
Then he yawned
                    and went to bed.

And if he met Gran on the stairs,
Good day, was what he said.

All the Dogs

You should have seen him—
he stood in the park and whistled,
underneath an oak tree,
and all the dogs came bounding up
and sat around him,
keeping their big eyes on him,
tails going like pendulums.
And there was one cocker pup
who went and licked his hand,
and a labrador who whimpered
till the rest joined in.
Then he whistled a second time,
high-pitched as a stoat,
over all the shouted dog names
and whistles of owners,
till a flurry of paws
brought more dogs, panting,
as if they'd come miles,
and these too found space
on the flattened grass
to stare at the boy's
unmemorable face
which all the dogs found special.

Me and Benjy

Me and Benjy, my teddybear,
went to bed to sleep.
What else would we do but sleep?
We couldn't, however—
the noise was atrocious,
shouting and laughing,
thumping and whooping—
Just imagine if that was us,
I whispered in Benjy's ear,
Guzzling wine and beer,
making one hell of a fuss!
What are we going to do?
I looked into Benjy's eyes,
Benjy's brownglass eyes.
Benjy, it has to be you,
I said, throwing him out,
then sliding out myself,
knocking a book from a shelf
with a thump, and a shout
from downstairs: *Go to sleep!*
The cheek of it, I thought.
One of their party ought
to investigate sleep-
possibilities up here,
to lie down on our bed,
pull the pillow over her head,
and ignore down there!
Come on Benjy, let's go.
We crept down the stairs,
me and that Benjybear,
and walked on tiptoe

to the living-room din
that vibrated the floor.
I pulled open the door
and chucked Benjy in.

Mule

Somewhere in Indo-China
a sick man is strapped
to a three-legged mule.

His name is Aloysius,
his memory is used up
but the mule knows.

With each hop-step
down the dirt road
the man cries out.

The mule sees the city
through the miles of trees
and the many nights

for the mule never sleeps,
keeps hop-stepping on
with his feverish man.

When he gets tired
birdwinged butterflies
sip at his eyes.

When he feels lonely
troops of parrots
flash overhead.

All through the nights
the hospital lights
burn in the sky,

with the moon the theatre
where the surgeon waits.
The mule knows.

While I Practise My Piano

I'm being haunted by child spirits.
The door keeps opening.
Will you sit in the room with me
while I practise my piano?
You can even sing—
they won't like that,
your voice would send a bee
careering into a wall,
or would start a cat wailing.
There's the door again,
why are you so slow
at getting in here?
I've got to keep playing—
else the child spirits
will take over my piano
and play tunes of their own,
tunes that might scare me,
and once they got going
they'd never stop, so
please keep me company,
please sit in the room with me
while I practise my piano.

Smile

Smile, go on, smile!
Anyone would think, to look at you,
that your cat was on the barbecue
or your best friend had died.
Go on, curve your mouth.
Take a look at that beggar,
or that one-legged bus conductor,
Where's *your* cross?
Smile, slap your thigh.
Hiccup, make a horse noise,
lollop through the house,
fizz up your coffee.
Take down your guitar
from its air-shelf and play
imaginary reggae
out through the open door.
And smile, remember, smile,
give those teeth some sun,
grin at everyone,
do it now, go on, SMILE!

The Unlit Suburbs

THE SUBMERGED BAR

Let's have a beer tonight
in the bar of the submerged town

where the drinks are all self-serve
and the last bell's never rung

and the music on the jukebox
hasn't been changed for years

and the beer's still at 60s prices
and no one smokes in there

and no policeman comes knocking
in the middle of the night

but it's best not to be found there
during the hours of daylight.

Rat Town

Beneath the bridge is rat town
and don't go there on your own

or they'll have your cheeks for starters,
your well-stuffed stomach for the main,

and littering the ground in rat town
are numerous bones like your own.

The Ghost Choir

The clarinet is playing through the ruined church,
gathering the ghosts to stand in the choir

and rescue from their deaths the voices they had,
which they send soaring, swooping on the wind

and each ghost remembers the coffin stood there.
the relatives weeping, the secret of the light.

The Long-Legged Chair

She bought a long-legged chair
and painted it red. And no one
but her could sit there,
head at the highest pane,
above the pictures of Marilyn,
above the mirror. She ate there,
fed herself boiled eggs,
babytalking all the while.
Sometimes she'd rock so hard
she'd almost fall. She liked
to listen to Mozart up there,
holding her head in her hands.
She went out less and less
and had no one round. Friends
gave up calling the ansaphone
that she heard from the chair,
then nothing, not a ring.
Once the doorbell went
but she was asleep up there,
woke to stare at the door,
seeing the cup-hook
and the judo-belt hanging
at just the height of the chair.

Sleep With A Suitcase

I slept with a suitcase last night.
It didn't snore. It was half-packed
and there was a map on the floor.
Outside, snow covered the roof
of my tanked-up car. I kept
my clothes on and the heating up,
and the phone off the hook.
I wanted no one and nothing
between me and the morning.
I set my alarm for the dawn.
The poison I fed the cat
was working in the dark kitchen.
The mailbox was in the trash.
I left a note on the oven
saying I was dead, forgotten,
and the house was my son's.
He would sleep for three days
then wake with a headache.
I left him aspirin and water,
and his father's phone number,
or the last one I knew.

Riding Into Town

The whistle of the bottle through the air,
the double-smash of glass, the screaming—
all this went through him like a breath,
in and out of his switched-off ears.
He was riding his horse through the town,
he didn't care what went on there—
the drunks taking chairs to each other,
the women in leggings, the policemen.

He had come here to smash the arms
of the statue that guarded the graveyard—
the statue of Our Lady of Prague
that had stood here since he was a kid.
With the noise, no one would hear him,
and no one came here after dark.
He peered skywards, and fondled the head
of the sledge concealed in his greatcoat.

Grandpa's Bed

My granny was my ally.
She'd help me out the window
and leave it open.
She didn't mind how long
I stayed, or what I did.
I could have slept with you
in her bed. Instead
I'd jump to the ground
and make for the graveyard,
lit by its one streetlight
on the edge of town.
It would be locked, of course,
but a pig had bent two bars
trying to get in. I'd creep
round the back of the church,
then, in the dark, I'd count
tombstones until my fingers
spelt out Grandpa's name.
While I waited, I told him
everything about you,
and asked his permission
to do what we did above him.
Then you'd arrive, shivering
even though it was summer,
whispering this was madness,
till we went down on Grandpa's bed.

Writing To A Dead Man

i.m. Raymond Tyner

I want to write to a dead man.
I want to recommend a book,
and slip in a potted 5-year history
of the world since him. I see him,
when I close my eyes, in a hammock—
that old Rastafarian hammock—
on our roof garden. He's naked
and reading Schopenhauer, with a cold
beer on the floor. He hears
an aircraft noise, then a voice
through a megaphone—a police voice,
telling him to get some clothes on.
He wrote me this in dudgeon
and did I answer? I want to
tell him I've sat in a car outside
the house he lived in, and eaten
in his favourite Chinese restaurant,
and heard the ignominious stories
of his last weeks—sleep in the office,
no home, linen hanging to dry
in full view of students. I recall
telephone conversations of that time,
his plans that could have included
burial on the moon, his riches
banked in his head. I reckon now
he'll be over that. Five years
in the earth of Georgia would cure that.
I'm sure of it. I want to tell him
I don't hold his last months against him,
and I think of him when I eat salmon,
and I now agree with him about Swift,

and he was wrong about Ireland,
about my coldness there, after we'd
visited Lisadell, and the Tower,
and stood at Yeats' grave. I want
to argue with him, gently,
and the best way is in a letter.
I know he saw ghosts in our flat
but I don't want to see him.
I don't mind that he won't write back.

Meat

I sent a pig's head to my mother-in-law.
A week later I sent two cows' eyes in a box.
I gave her no clue of my identity,
and didn't tell my wife. She heard soon enough—
a crying on the phone halfway through dinner,
and I choked on a boar sausage, laughing,
while my wife turned round and glared.

It was like good mustard when she told me.
As she spoke I knew what I'd send next—
lambs' testicles. One by one I'd send her mother
all my grandfather's favourites: snipe, rabbit,
ox tail, chitterlings and blood from a pig.
I hoped she hadn't thrown out her recipes.
How did she think she could renounce meat?

Chinese Opera

for Charles Simic

She lit the sky with her own fireworks show
at 4 a.m. Up there on her roofgarden,
in her moon & stars dressing gown
she drained the last of the champagne
then struck the first match. Downstairs,
in the living room, Chinese opera was playing—
the last gift he'd given her with a grin.
She'd played that tape non-stop since then.

He'd laughed until she'd started joining in
with thin quivery vowels stretched and bent,
sobs and cymbal-bashes, and dialogue
spoken in English—her own translations
which varied every time but always
had broken or sacrificed men—and laments
sung in her improvised Chinese, like now
on the roof as she sent the rockets high.

Our Ikky

He's up in the air again,
our Ikky, but he won't get far—
no crow's black wings
are as ramshackle as his,
though they're the third of the year
and the best yet. Bald hens,
broken window frames,
nails, and string, and glue,
leather, sawn plastic bottles,
green crocodile balloons—
all these helped Ikky's wings
get Ikky up in the air.
But he's not going to stay there.
Last time he got ten yards,
as far as the allotments.
He crashed into a weed fire
and saw turnips. The first time
he never got off the ground.
Look at him now, a giant insect
from Mars, legs dangling,
blue swimming goggles on.
'Ikky, watch out for that plane!'
'Ikky, have you got
your parachute on? Will I
call the hospital?' No sound
from Ikky, as he rises
over the pit museum
and heads for the North Sea.
Will he do it this time, Ikky?

Will he make Helsinki?
I wish him gull-staying-power,
I wish him no sun but wind.

The Mules

One of them was lame when they bought him
but a rest and a bandage saw to that,
then a week of parsnips and sugar
had him whinnying for the valley,
up which his comrades would canter
at least once daily, carrying panniers
of lemons and olives, newspapers, bread,
goats' milk for the allergic, medicines,
incense, wine for the doctors,
and once a consignment of used Amstrads
that the mules would never forget.
They didn't mind the twisting narrow lanes
that rose from the valley. Even when snow
kept the postman at sea-level,
they slithered down to the village,
and all three of them got used to the hands
of the gentler patients, stroking them
as they stood there chomping daffodils,
or peeing on flagstones, or sleeping
standing up, oblivious to problems
with striking nurses, ward revolts,
doctor burn-outs, or the RAF manoeuvres
that exploded the sky above them.
There were worse outposts for a mule.

Donkey Hoof

A donkey hoof makes the best brooch.
It also makes an excellent soup
and left in the sun, then crumbled,
it is the only true aphrodisiac.
Two donkey hooves mean luck at poker
but three mean a month in hospital,
and anything over three means death.

Ancient Egypt rubbed crushed hoof
into bald heads. I have no record
of its success, but I'm sure it worked.
All a Celtic cowherd needed
was a donkey hoof and a donkey poem
and a young donkey was there to jump on.
A donkey hoof is the best currency.

Hollowed out, a hoof will float—
give one to your favourite toddler.
The lightest donkeys walk on water.
The world is crammed in a donkey hoof.
Petition NASA to blast one up
and loose it among the space debris.

Dancer

Dancing round the pond, she attracted
an audience of men, half-drunk, mainly,
spilling out of the pub to shout
'Take them off, luvvy, what little you've left'
or 'Give us a feel, gorgeous, go on'
or 'If you jump in I'll jump in and save you'.
She paid no more attention to any of them
than she did to the moon or its reflection
or all the miles of black air in between.
Someone began humming a homemade song
that fitted her dancing. Another danced after her,
out of step, unsteady, liable to fall in.
Cars slowed down and stopped, horns blew,
drivers whistled, but she carried on dancing
round and round, steady as a swimmer,
neither fast nor slow, head erect,
and none of the men blocked her path
or dared to approach, and touch her,
not even when, at last, she wheeled away
and danced out of sight, down the hill.

The Dog

He was walking an imaginary dog.
He'd stop and yank an invisible lead,
turning to growl at the creature
that he hadn't got all day, that no dog
needed to pee every five yards,
than any minute now rain would fall
from a sky as blue as his one eye.

He brought the dog into the pub.
He tied it to the leg of a chair,
got a pint of stout and sat there
as I followed him in, pretending
to look for someone, then sitting down
with a beer of my own, to stare at him
talking to the dog and to himself.

He drained his glass and got another.
He leaned down and stroked the dog,
muttering to it things I couldn't hear,
straightening up to smile to himself,
then I had to go, out into the November
sunlight, looking behind me, listening
for the faintest whimper or bark.

Postcards

Sailed to Normandy in an afternoon haze,
peered out the window and drank some wine,
saw a dead gull floating on the Channel
and a piece of wood from a broken boat.
Thought of the postcards I could make of those,
how a market was there for cards of the dead—
planecrashes in Andean forests, hidden by leaves;
space-debris; the skeleton of a horse;
a wrecked tank in a Sarajevan suburb;
a pile of clothes left on an empty beach—
nothing as crude as a mutilated body.
I'd keep all my cards black and white
and limit them to a numbered hundred.
Yes, I could see them covering the wall
of the sitting-room I'd hacked out of a cave
on the de-inhabited island I'd bought
with the proceeds of their sale. Around me
ruined crofts, rabbits zapped by myxomatosis,
a lighthouse that last shone in the 20s,
and the north wind blowing me to bone.

Skylight

When I stand under it
I feel like a fish in winter
looking up through ice.

This defector from a greenhouse,
this window that wandered,
wanting to be neither horizontal nor vertical,
is my favourite. Bay windows,
French windows, portholes—you can keep them.
I don't want to see mountains.
I like *paintings* of waves.

Only the clouds excite me
with their ceaseless messages—
I learned first of the Gulf War
when I read a cloud.
I successfully warned a chef friend
to avoid a consignment of king prawns
that poisoned a rival's clientele.

Sometimes I photograph clouds through glass.

I heard a knocking once, hard,
as on a door, but when I got up there
the visitor was gone.

Keep Him In

Keep him back, don't let him out.
Lock the door, keep him in overnight,
make him cover the greenboard
in writing so small he'll need
a magnifying glass or a telescope
to help him read it back to us.
Leave him different coloured chalks.

Advise him to write in stanzas.
Switch the heating off, but grant him
a half-filled electric kettle,
coffee, and maybe a sandwich.
Call him hourly, to check progress.
(Have a blues playing in the background.)
Tell him he's good, shudderingly good.

Tell him, on the 5th or 6th call,
there's whiskey in the bottom drawer,
but warn him you can't write drunk.
He'll know that, he's turned 40.
Don't hassle him, don't ask what
his lines are about. You'll know
when he reads them out in the a.m.

And you'll have the tape switched on
while you whack him on the back.
His best work, no doubt about it!
Already you glimpse the Russian version.
You know a woodcut for the cover.
Let him out now, call him a cab.
It wouldn't do to overwork him.

The Attic

I've finished my mural of you naked,
and only I will see it.
The sun streams through the skylight,
lighting your face, your breasts.
I lie in the hammock remembering
the afternoon hours I spent with you
up here, where no one goes.
We'd have Van Morrison singing
low down, and sometimes wine.
Always there'd be a vase of flowers
in the corner, on the trunk—
you'd smuggle them up the stairs
until you closed that black door
and the rest of the house wasn't there.
I remember the day we fell asleep
until they came looking for us—
my mother calling my name,
but not coming up. We waited
till all was quiet, then reappeared
in the living room, and sat apart,
like we had to, for half an hour—
the longest you spent down there—
then I went with you to the door.
I wouldn't accompany you to the bus stop,
instead went back upstairs
to lie there in the growing dark,
listening to Van over and over again.
I must have known you'd never return.
It was weeks before I started the mural,
and I took my time, I wanted *you* there,
on my wall, right in every detail,

looking as if I could lift you down.
I wanted you, and now I've got you
and you'll never go downstairs.
Tomorrow I'll paint a vase of flowers,
irises, to match your eyes,
but tonight I'm sleeping here,
the first night I'll have spent with you.

The Houseboat

'Did Dick Blackstaff do it?
Is he the fucker we want?'
We banged on the hatch of that houseboat,
under a blood-red moon,
while a police siren weaved among the flats
and a dog howled till a shot rang out.
But we heard no sound from the cabin,
no whisper, or muffled step,
so we banged again, and shouted
'Blackstaff, if you're in there
come out and clear your name.'
And these words rang over the water
to the wreck of the tanker
where the kids hung out in summer
but now was as bare as a crag.
And the houseboat rocked, as the wind
whipped up the incoming tide,
and brought with it the smell of curry
from *The Star of Malibar*.
'Tell Blackstaff there's a bullet
waiting for his skull,' we shouted
before jumping back to land
and cramming in Jack's Audi
for the short ride home.

Weddings And Funerals

Or poem beginning with a line by John Hartley Williams

In those days I didn't go to weddings.
All that noisy drinking got me down
and chicken and ham with mushy vegetables
was best eaten once a year at most.
I hated the homegrown country music
that dragged everyone to the dance floor,
and even more the yelps and squeals
when the bride was twirled by the groom,
but worst of all was the leering question
when was it going to be my turn?

No one asked that at the funerals
I took to hunting out and attending,
and the black jacket and jeans I wore
got nods of approval and sad smiles.
I loved the stately walking rhythms
as we shuffled after the coffins,
inside of which were mostly strangers,
and I always managed a graveside tear
which earned me a beer and a sandwich
in the hotel later, where no one danced.

A Day In Calcutta

The flesh of the Indian mango is red
    like a pawpaw
but the taste is all mango.
I had it for breakfast one morning
    with watermelon juice
in that sumptuous hotel in Calcutta
    before heading off
in one of those 50s Rovers
through the crazy beeping streets
    to visit the temple
of Kalighat. It was early
    but already
there were plenty of would-be guides,
the least insistent of which we chose
    to lead us
barefoot, into Kali's sanctum
    where hands pushed us
up to her idol (black goddess
with fierce red eyes, looking as if,
    despite being stone,
she could tear us into pieces),
    as ochre marks
were thumbed on our foreheads
and offerings were requested,
    More, more
you rich Westerner! . . . Eventually
    we were outside
and heading back to our shoes
when I saw, in a crowd of men,
    two tethered goats,
one young, one a baby, both

big-eyed and curious,
especially the eldest, until grabbed
at both ends, his neck stretched,
then a flash
of a knife and his head was in the dust.
The younger's bleats
were cut short in the same way,
and both bodies were dragged
over the ground
(getting blood on my feet) and away.
I shrugged off
the demands for money, caught up with
the others, and climbed back in
the 50s Rover
to join the maelstrom of traffic again,
the constant beeping
and weaving across lanes,
the certain collisions avoided,
jaywalkers dodged
with that special skill that's the mark
of Calcutta,
till I ended up in the leafy calm
of the British cemetery, where the Raj
has never ended,
or so I thought, until I strolled—
reading the names
and epitaphs—to the far end
where Indian boys were playing cricket
among the tombs.

The Horses

Or poem beginning with a line from Kafka's Diaries

A herd of horses broke out of the enclosure
and galloped furiously down the dusty road.

Their leader was a sleek black stallion
with one white star gleaming on his brow.

At the edge of town they clattered onto tarmac,
tore past the church like a flooding river,

then, without slowing down, squeezed closer
to surge between the banks of parked cars.

Anyone caught driving put the boot down
on seeing that lot crowding the rear mirror

and one fat man who couldn't cross in time
felt a hoof burst his belly before he fainted.

The last in the stampede was a skinny colt,
increasingly adrift from the others,

but who still kept going, through red lights,
game as any straggler in the National,

and no one stood on the pavement with a lasso
trying to stop this last one from fleeing.

By the time the colt passed the bingo hall
the stallion had progressed beyond the graveyard

and soon all that was seen of the herd
was a cloud of dust moving above the foothills.

The too-quick dusk took away even that
and the search was called off a week later.

My Daughter And Ray Davies

She's going out again to that pub in Muswell Hill,
her and that bass-guitarist boyfriend of her's,
and she's wearing those red velvet hipsters.

It's not the 134 she's taking, it's a time machine.
Look at her hair, it's a disgrace. Mods are gone,
I say, but she smiles. She's on her way to Ray Davies.

I don't know what he sees in the pair of them,
or why he listens to tapes of the boyfriend's band—
him, the writer of 'Lola' and 'You Really Got Me'.

Her room is a Kinks' shrine—all my records
nicked, and pride of place on the wall,
a blown-up photo of the three of them together.

She knows I'd love to come on the bus with them,
go down with Ray (and maybe Dave) to his local,
chat about the 60s, about the bands then,

but even though I'm younger than Ray, it's not on—
might as well try to get into the boyfriend's band,
so I sneak back my Kinks records while she's gone

and play them so loud the neighbours complain,
while she's laughing at Ray's latest jokes,
knocking back the cider to his whisky and beer.

Five Fighters

Strung out on the neon horizon,
the five fighters approached,
two to the left, two to the right
and one above Canary Wharf.
The searchlights and sirens were obsolete
or not yet updated, and no one
could make out the fuselage markings
so couldn't know where they came from
or why they were here,
as they cut across Southwark,
crossed the Thames for the second time
to buzz the Houses of Parliament—
policemen running, sirens bansheeing
but no tracer from rattatting guns.
Then they banked and veered to the north,
past Covent Garden and Holborn,
past Hackney and Chigwell
into deepest, darkest Essex
where they disappeared into the sky,
and none of those who'd seen them
was sure anymore, but who
wouldn't have visions of the night
the five fighters swooped on London,
flew into the centre and out again
without one of them firing a shot?

Hooves

The sound of galloping hooves woke me,
then a high, lengthy whinny
pulled me out of bed to the window
to see a horse standing there,
his long, black head over my gate.

There was a fine saddle on his back
with no one in it. He stared up,
never taking his eyes off mine,
as if he was mine, and I'd forgotten.
I'd have to get dressed and go out to him.

I didn't know what to do with horses,
but I took a towel with me,
and water. He'd be hot and sweaty.
Maybe I should lead him down to the sea,
so he could swim for a few minutes.

As I towelled his neck he neighed
and I smelled rescue remedy on his breath,
a smell I knew far too well.
Who'd given him that? Who'd sent
him here, and for what reason?

Was I, who'd never been on a horse,
supposed to climb into that saddle,
and let him take me where he would?
It was too cold out here to think.
I needed a strong black coffee.

I couldn't just leave the horse, though.
I wanted to take him into the house
but he was too big. Besides,
what would he do if he got in—
throw himself down on the sofa?

I tried to slink off up the steps
but his big eyes, as I turned round,
made me feel like a torturer,
so I got my scarf and leather jacket,
locked the door and got on the horse.

Immediately, he swung away,
trotting to begin with, then increasing
to a slowish gallop. I clung on,
eyes closed, clutching the horse's neck,
as his hooves rang on the road to Aldeburgh.

The Sleeping Sailor

Under the upturned boat
lay a sailor.
He wasn't dead, only sleeping—
sleeping off a night of rum.
When he'd staggered back from the pub
it had been raining
so he'd turned over the boat
and climbed inside.
Out on the bay his ship waited.
Already the Captain paced his cabin,
muttering to the walls.
When the first rays of sunlight
sparkled on the bay—
and all the rain left the sky
and an early dog came sniffing,
then barking at the boat—
the sailor woke.
His head hurt.
His mouth was dry.
He cursed the dog,
heaved the boat right way up,
dragged it to the water,
gathered his oars
and began to row.
An eye at the end of a telescope
watched him approach,
and underneath it a grim smile grew.

Maggot Song

Loosely taken from the Icelandic Creation Myth, 'Edda'

We are the giant maggots,
the squirmy tent-poles of the world.

We are *North*, *South*, *East* and *West*.
Together we hold up the sky.

Our mouth-hooks sink into clouds.
Our tails poke into the ground.

Between us, around us, the great wind
broadcasts our maggot song.

And I am North, my tail's in ice,
I have never shed my frozen skin.

I am South, my ice is colder,
cold as the meteorites I gobble.

I am East, I'm the Doctor Maggot,
My patient's the Ozone Layer.

And I am West, my tail must dance
when the earth shakes and cracks.

We are the giant maggots,
we're older than all the seas.

We're invisible, un-get-riddable.
Without us you wouldn't be.

We breathe through our mouths,
we breathe through our bums.

Between us, around us, the great wind
broadcasts our maggot song.

Permissions

'All the Dogs', 'Fishbones Dreaming', 'The Flying Spring Onion', 'Johnjoe's Snowman', 'Me and Benjy', 'Mule' and 'Night Boy' from *The Flying Spring Onion* (Faber and Faber, 1992). Copyright © Matthew Sweeney. Reprinted by permission of the publisher.

'Smile' and 'While I Practise My Piano' from *Fatso in the Red Suit* (Faber and Faber, 1995). Copyright © Matthew Sweeney. Reprinted by permission of the publisher.

'A Day in Calcutta', 'The Attic', 'Five Fighters', 'Hooves', 'The Horses', 'The Houseboat', 'My Daughter and Ray Davies' and 'Weddings and Funerals' from *A Smell of Fish* (Jonathan Cape, 2000). Copyright © Matthew Sweeney. Reprinted by permission of the publisher.